THE
HANGOVER
SURVIVAL GUIDE

Ken & Mahon —
After All Of The
Margaritas, This
Should Help!

12·2014

david l. sloan   christopher shultz

Phantom Press
Key West, Florida

This page would normally contain a bunch of legal mumbo jumbo, but we are feeling a bit hungover. Don't sue us, we won't sue you. If you want to use book excerpts in flattering newspaper articles, go ahead. If you are thinking of posting it on the Internet so everyone can read it for free, please don't. If you are in desperate need of a real copyright page, tear one out of another book and paste it in here. They all look pretty much the same.

If you are still reading this, we are impressed. Most people skip right past this page or only read the first sentence. It's your book now, do with it as you wish. We thought it would be cool to put subliminal messages throughout the book urging everyone to buy more copies. We didn't do it, but it would have been cool. Maybe you can tell everyone to buy two copies. You're still reading this so it's not like you have anything else to do. You can be our word of mouth advertising and for that we will tell you a joke. A man was putting on his tuxedo when his daughter came running up to him. "Don't wear that daddy. It always gives you a headache the next day." Enjoy the book!

Please address inquiries to:
Phantom Press
1025 Roberts Lane
Key West, FL 33040

Cover Design: WoduMedia.com
Page Layout: Kerry Karshna
Editing: Mandy Bolen
Photos: roboneal.com

ISBN 0-9674498-8-X
10 9 8 7 6 5 4 3 2 1 Blast Off

Printed in the USA

"Always do sober what you said you'd do drunk.
That will teach you to keep your mouth shut."

~ Ernest Hemingway

THE
HANGOVER
SURVIVAL GUIDE

david l. sloan   **christopher shultz**

Phantom Press
Key West, Florida

If this page is signed by Chris and David, your book will be worth lots of money when they are dead.

What'll It Be?

What'll It Be?

We raise our glasses...

To the Key West bartenders
Who make us feel fine,
Serving our liquor, our beer and our wine.
You call us our taxi,
You help us with dates.
You open up early,
And close really late.
You give us a handshake,
A wink or a nod.
All while mixing Manhattans,
Or sometimes Cape Cods.
We would like to say thank you,
You are the best.
And such a big part,
Of our lives in Key West.
How can we thank you
Apart from the tips,
And that Fantasy Fest
When we lent you our whips?
If we were bartenders,
We would buy you a brew.
But alas we are writers,
So this book's for you!

~David and Chris

roboneal.com
David and Chris appear courtesy of yo' mama

David Sloan
Get your own "free beer tomorrow" sign at Montage on Duval Street.

One for the road.

A sick joke for sick people

You are probably familiar with a story that dominated headlines in the mid 1980s about a boy who was born without a body. His name was Patrick Stanley, and though he had no torso, arms, legs or chest to speak of, the boy had a biological makeup that baffled doctors and scientists and allowed him to survive with only a head; a simple beautiful noggin. Patrick's parents shunned the initial publicity that accompanied their decision to keep the head… errr, boy, and with the fall of the Berlin Wall the media focused their attention elsewhere so the Stanleys went about raising their son the best way they knew how.

The first few years were the toughest. Medical bills and doctors visits nearly crippled the family financially. On top of that there were neighbors who turned their backs on them and churches who labeled Patrick "The Demon Child" or "Head of Satan." It was not easy for poor Patrick, but the Stanley's held their heads high and gave Patrick more love than any child could hope for.

It was January of 2005 when Patrick made headlines again. It was his 21st birthday so his father took him to Key West for a proper celebration. They had just watched the sun go down at Mallory Square when Mr. Stanley surprised his son by taking him to a Duval Street bar for his very first beer. The people of Key West did not find anything odd about a young man with no body, but when they heard he had just turned 21, a crowd gathered to help Patrick celebrate.

The bartender poured him an ice cold draft and set it on the bar. Patrick's father lifted the mug to his son's lips, and as Patrick

"A hangover is when you open your eyes in the morning and wish that you hadn't."
~ Andy Capp

took a sip his head jumped up from the bar and a neck popped out. The bar patrons stared in amazement as Mr. Stanley raised the glass again and a shoulder and arm popped out from the newly grown neck.

Mr. Stanley cried tears of happiness and ordered another beer, encouraging Patrick to drink so more limbs could grow. Pop! Pop! Another arm and a torso suddenly appeared. Pop! Pop! Two legs with feet and toes came out. No one could believe their eyes and the bar whooped and applauded as Patrick stood from the bar and took his first steps. It had taken nearly eight beers, but he was walking. The boy was walking.

Heavily buzzed, Patrick worked his way across the room – no easy task with new legs and 96 ounces of beer in your bloodstream. Suddenly he slipped, stumbled and fell through the large open windows to the sidewalk outside. The momentum from the spill kept him rolling into the street where he was run over and killed by a tomato delivery truck.

The bar patrons stood in silence, too shocked by the series of events to say a word. The bartender finally broke the silence, putting his hand on Mr. Stanley's shoulder and offering words of condolence, "I guess he should have quit while he was a head!"

You may be upset that you exerted so much energy reading the above paragraphs only to be rewarded with a cheesy joke. Fair enough, but before you toss this book in the corner you should know that you threw up in that corner last night and nobody will want to read your book if it is covered in vomit. You should also know that the best way to avoid a hangover is to quit

while you are ahead. We don't care much for moderation in the Keys, so instead of telling you not to drink, we are going to give you a heaping helping of advice on how to make the most of your Key West hangover. Start saving up your energy, it's almost time to turn the page.

Henrietta Jigsaw
Visit Patrick Stanley's headstone at the Key West Cemetery

"The easiest way to avoid a hangover
is to stay drunk."
~ Unknown

roboneal.com
Manic Monkey appears courtesy of the Flying Spaghetti Monster

How's It Hanging?
The Key West hangover defined

Congratulations on making it to the second chapter. Maybe that hangover isn't quite as bad as you thought. Now, go stick your head under the faucet of the bathroom sink and drink as much water as you can possibly handle. The fridge is empty and we are about to give you an exciting little education on how you came to feel like a half dead, alcoholic puffer fish.

Word Up!

An overhang is something that extends beyond something else, such as a roof going over a porch. In your case the "something" would be the effects of alcohol and the "something else" would be the time you spent at the bar actually thinking you would get lucky. Leave it to drinkers to screw up a word. Overhang was reversed and turned into hangover, but we only call it that because "veisalgia" is too difficult to pronounce when a tequila worm is gnawing away at your cerebral cortex. What is "veisalgia," you ask. Read on.

Greeks, Geeks and Vikings:

Veisalgia is the term those geeky guys who blew off frat parties to pursue a degree in science have given to the hangover. Leave it people who don't drink to name the hangover with an unpronounceable word. While we were busy running around in togas maintaining the Greek traditions, these losers were learning the Greek language. They took the term "algia" which means pain,

About one in 10 people older than 21 experience
a hangover after only one or two drinks.

combined it with the Norwegian Viking term "kveis" meaning "uneasiness following debauchery," jumbled the two words together and invented a new word describing more symptoms than you will find in back to back commercials for Nyquil and Pepto Bismol. Those geeks know how to have a good time, but they are unlikely to suffer of the symptoms you know so well.

Island Fever?

How's your veisalgia hanging? Headache, sensitivity to light and sound, diarrhea, fatigue and nausea are just a few of the symptoms you may be experiencing. If you really did a number on yourself, these may be accompanied by increased heart rate, dehydration, trouble concentrating, anxiety, a poor sense of overall well being and the desire to die quickly. Regretting the night before? Throw in a rooster crowing four feet from your bedroom window and you are one step closer to a full-fledged Key West hangover. Cayo Huesoveisalgia for you scientists geeks.

Our Spirited Past:

Key West is a town where hangovers have history, so it would be safe to say that alcohol is in our blood. Would you expect anything less from an island first inhabited by Indians? Ponce de Leon put Key West on the map during his quest for the ultimate drink, but the Indians were enjoying the island's liquid libations long before his arrival. Proof can be found at the Heritage House on Caroline Street where a fresh water well, once used by

Indians, still remains. Though they only came to drink water, what do you suppose was going on the night before that made them so desperate for this water in the first place? It is a safe bet that fire water was involved, and there were probably some peace pipes too. We are no experts on history, but this would explain why the next set of explorers found the Indians' remains scattered about the trees. Such a gruesome sight certainly led to more drinking, and before you knew it, the rumrunners were setting up shop and the pirates were partying down. Word traveled fast about the crazy-ass parties in Key West and as time went on we had over three million people coming down here each year to kick off their shoes and drink the booze in search of the Key West Hangover.

My Kind of Town:

Key West is a drinking town. We finish late, we start early and we try not to judge. The island has a festive, tropical atmosphere with an attitude that is conducive to drinking. The real world seems to disappear below the horizon with the sun and the drinks flow like water in more than fifty bars on Duval Street alone. People drink more in Key West than they do in most cities and this leads to hangovers of new magnitude. There are hangovers and there are Key West hangovers. Take the test and see which you have. Here are some hangover thoughts from Key West locals to get you in the mood.

The average number of drinks that causes
hangover symptoms is **3.2**

Ask The Locals

Anywhere you go, locals know best. Here is what some of our island's experts had to say about Key West hangovers.

"You can call in hungover...At least where I work."
~ John Besh ~ Finnegan's Wake

"The worst thing about a Key West hangover is realizing the cool thing on your head is the toilet. "
~ Eli Pancamo

"I do it. I do it a lot and I don't like it."
~Brant Northgate

"A Key West hangover...Just another day in paradise."
~Steve Calderwood

"A Key West hangover...I thought that was ordinary."
~Vil Vilips

"Eating a bunch of bananas and howling from the top of a Poinciana tree."
~Alice, the monkey of Key West's Alice

roboneal.com
Kim Sklar appears courtesy of Kim Sklar Productions

1. The taste in my mouth is best described as:
   a. Fresher than the Prince of Bel Air.
   b. Mmmm. Pizza.
   c. There are socks on my teeth that taste like three-day-old oatmeal.
   d. When I catch the cat that crapped in my mouth I am going to eat him.
   e. Ai cownt moo ma toong.

2. The sensation in my head is like:
   a. Bluebirds and bunnies playing in the breeze.
   b. I think it is thumping to the beat of "Girl from Ipanema."
   c. The drum solo from "In a gada davida."
   d. I need aspirin. Give me the damn bottle.
   e. Shut up. SHUT UP. SHUUUT UUUUUUUP!!!

3. Mention of a greasy pork sandwich in a dirty ashtray makes me:
   a. Hungry for lunch and a cigarette.
   b. I don't eat pork and I gave up smoking.
   c. That's not nice. I don't like you
   d. If you put down the quiz to hurl circle d.
   e. If your vomit was accompanied by explosive diarrhea at the same time circle e.

I envy people who are hungover.
At least they have something to blame everything on.

4. My hair:
   a. Gee, my hair smells terrific and fresh.
   b. Stinks like cigarettes and beer.
   c. Looks like Sid Vicious on acid.
   d. Is caked with puke and hurts when I touch it.
   e. My hair is…where is it? What the hell happened to my hair?

5. For a bottle of water, I would be willing to:
   a. Take a walk to the store and pay fair market value.
   b. I'll buy, you fly. Pick me up a bag of Cool Ranch Doritos.
   c. Stop playing games and give me the frickin' water.
   d. Here's twenty bucks. Can you get the cap off for me?
   e. I will kill my mother and eat my first born child alive for a spit of liquid in my rotten, festering mouth.

6. On a scale of 1-10 I would rate my hangover:
   a. 1
   b. 3
   c. 7
   d. 9
   e. 346

IslandJoesGourmetCoffee.com

IN THE KNOW WITH ISLAND JOE!
At one time in England, certain merchants were angered when coffee was introduced. Those selling ale and wine felt threatened when coffee became more popular. They even launched a campaign to persuade Charles II to issue an order to suppress coffeehouses. Fortunately, public outcry forced the order to be retracted. That was on January 8, 1675.

WE HAVE THE ANSWERS!

Mostly A: No one told us the Mormons were in town. We've always wanted to visit the Tabernacle! Anyway, it looks like a good beach day for you, but there is work to be done. Get your cheer-ass down to the store and pick up some water for the people trying to keep the good bartenders of Key West in business. And stop whistling, it's annoying.

Mostly B: You have not even begun to understand the meaning of pain. Drink some Evian, brush your teeth and head on down to the Schooner Wharf Bar. Befriend the locals and challenge them to a drinking contest. Be sure to ask Jerry about the bullfight, but don't mention the cockfight.

Mostly C: Not bad for an amateur. Continue drinking as usual tonight, but head to the Green Parrot before calling it quits and drink a half-dozen root beer barrels. Keep up the training and you will be Key West material in no time.

Mostly D: You made a valiant effort, but you are still a loser. Wallow in your sorrow then head for the Hog's Breath Saloon. Skip the beer and head straight for the hard stuff. It is going to be a long night to get to where you need to be.

Mostly E: Congratulations! You have a Key West hangover. Unfortunately you could give a rat's ass what kind of hangover you have and would obtain an equal amount of enjoyment from having a vegetable peeler jammed into your eyeball. At least it takes your mind off the headache. Take it easy. These next pages will help you ease the pain and prepare yourself better in the future.

roboneal.com
Don't even ask how we got Kim Sklar to pose for this one.
Hands courtesy of David Sloan.

roboneal.com
Bottle appears courtesy of Public Enemy

If you have a Key West hangover and are convinced of impending death but can't remember the number for 911, skip ahead to chapter six for some island remedies. The rest of you sissies need to prepare for battle. This is a war and it is a war we will win. There are bars on every corner, pretty girls lurking on stairways with ice cold drafts, street vendors with blenders and restaurants serving fine wines. We cannot avoid them, troops, but we can sample their delights and remain strong enough to wake up the next morning and face them again. We will fight them on the streets, we will fight them on the beaches, we will fight them on the champagne sunset sails and we will fight them in the bars. We will never surrender. This section will explain the cause of a Key West hangover in greater detail and prepare you to infiltrate the town with your fellow party animals so that victory is ours.

What Ales Ya?

This is the part where we tell you about things going in and out of your body. None of it will resemble the ins and outs of your porn collection unless you like being peed on. If that's the case; please keep it to yourself. Life is too short to be confused by large scientific terms, and dictionaries make bad hangover reading. We have taken the liberty of replacing these large scientific terms with hangover-friendly names to which you can relate. In this next section, "Vasopressin" will be referred to as "Oreos."

Outside of New Year's Eve, **43 %** of people said they're most likely to get a hangover after a wedding related event, such as a reception and bachelor or bachelorette parties.

Toss Your Cookies:

If you slam back a shot of tequila and manage to keep it from re-emerging on the bar, your little Mexican friend will enter the bloodstream and make a beeline for your brain. Once there, he will pull a gun on your pituitary gland and say, "Stop making Oreos or I will kill you." The gland stops because he could care less about making Oreos. He'd much prefer a siesta with the Mexican. The problem is the rest of your body loves Oreos and needs Oreos. Especially the filling.

When the Oreos stop being produced, your kidneys get angry. Angry kidneys are bad. You see, it is the kidneys' job to re-absorb water into the body. They are paid for their work with their favorite thing in the world – Oreos. Your kidneys love their Oreos so much that when the supply is cut off they say, "Screw this. No Oreos, no work. Let that lazy bladder do the job." With the kidneys on strike, all of the water scheduled for re-absorption in the kidneys goes straight to the bladder. The bladder hates extra work, but really has no choice. The extra water makes him pissed, so he sends signals to the brain complaining about the extra liquid. The brain is taking a siesta with the Mexican so he gets upset, and the end result is frequent trips to the bathroom. This leads to a broken seal, dehydration, an extremely large hangover and a nasty job for the guy who cleans the bathrooms. Holding back Oreos from the kidneys is like taking cookies from a pregnant woman. Anger, frustration, a violent headache and a lot of peeing is the result. Oreos keep your body and pregnant ladies calm and happy.

Strain on the Brain:

One shot of tequila makes your body expel four shots of water. Four shots of tequila expels sixteen shots of water, and ten shots of tequila expels your lunch. You will be too busy amazing the bar with your newfound wit and wisdom to notice the dehydration kicking in, but your body knows. Your body always knows. As you pass out in your socks without drinking a bottle of water, your organs start freaking out like those small farming towns you see praying for rain in the movies. When the rain doesn't come, the organs get nasty and one of the smarter organs starts an uprising just like that girl on "Survivor" did with the beef jerky. "The brain has water! He's holding out on us!" The organs form an alliance and start stealing all of the water from your undeserving brain. "What does he need water for anyways? He's been cheating us all along!" As the water is being lifted from your brain it shrinks, faster than usual, but his membranes are still attached to your skull, so it pulls away hard and your brain screams out, "Ouch! What the hell are you guys doing?" The organs reply, "Screw you. You shouldn't have stopped making Oreos." This is when you wake up from your slumber, stumble naked across the hardwood floor and do the slip and slide in your socks until you hit the floor. This is the time to take off your socks and call a truce in the body war by drinking a big bottle of water with the promise never to drink again.

Nearly three in five people who experience hangovers are likely to have one on New Year's day.

Pissed down the drain:

Your organs have been drained of water, your brain is attempting to detach itself from your skull, and your socks are stuck to your feet. What else could possibly go wrong? Do you vaguely remember the twenty trips to the bathroom last night? Your broken seal has not only exposed you to the countless germs in our public restrooms, but has freed your body of the basic nutrients it needs to survive.

Salts and potassium, required by your nerves and muscles to function properly, have been pissed away. You thought it was the asparagus that made your pee smell funny? Your constant whizzing has also exported magnesium and glycogen from your liver. The dispensing of these chemicals doesn't exactly make your body a happy camper. Weakness, fatigue, lack of coordination and depleted energy can be added to the list of your deteriorating state, and for one reason or another your cell function has been damaged as well.There are still no Oreos in sight and you did not get lucky, but all is not lost. These unfortunate side effects can be drastically reduced by taking the Key West Hangover Survival Guide's advice on preparing your body to handle this debauchery without going into a civil war. Read on.

Wet Nap:

Sleeping Beauty had plenty of rest. The wicked witch stayed awake all night with her brew. Which one would you rather sleep with?

Rest is very important, but Key West makes it extremely tough to sleep late or turn in early for fear of missing out on all of the fun. Bars open at 6 a.m. and close at 4 a.m. There are house parties, after-hours parties, booze cruises, beach bars, champagne brunches and happy hours. Drinks are always near and everyone seems to be on vacation. What is a drinker to do? We are guessing you have certain objectives while drinking. Whether it is meeting people, laughing, joking, dancing, sharing stories, catching a buzz or meeting members of the opposite sex, it all can be done with ease, but in order to meet most of these objectives you will need to be on top of your game. The island lifestyle may frown on stopping early or starting late, but we love our naps. We'll take one now while you read about the benefits of napping.

Better health, maximum alertness, improved mood and better looks are a few benefits of sleep. No one should bat an eyelash if you announce that you are going to take a nap. If they do, invite them to join you. If for some reason you are fearful of looking like a pansy for announcing nap time, just head to the beach, find a comfortable palm tree, pull your hat down and snooze away. Not in the mood for sand in your shorts? Grab a chair on a porch with a breeze or for the soundest sleep, join the homeless and get your rest at the Monroe County Library under the palm trees in

ISLAND JOE'S COFFEE SAYS:
When drinking where the smugglers ran, the best way to keep the energy up is with Smugglers' Brew. For those who like the sweet part of the dark side.

IslandJoesGourmetCoffee.com

the shaded garden. If anyone knows a good nap spot, it is the homeless. Thirty minutes of down time will get you two more hours in the bar, and an hour of rest will have you in it for the long run, vying for the title of Key West's Drinking Champion. Know the difference between napping and sleeping. It has been scientifically proven that more than an hour of sleep will screw up your cycle and you will be tired for the rest of the night. Stick to an hour of rest and you will have an air about you that makes it impossible to go home alone, unless you took a nap with the homeless and didn't bother to shower, of course. Now let's wake up from our naps and put our mats away. The Key West Hangover Survival Guide is proud to present another key factor in fighting your hangover. We're heading to Vitamin Street.

A to Zinc:

Funny how we won't think twice about spending eight bucks on a margarita, five bucks for a pack of cigarettes, and ten dollars for a cab ride, but the $6.49 bottle of One-A-Day Plus Iron does not fit our budget. Vitamins are an important factor when reducing the effects of an impending hangover and those magical little pills help fix everything you broke the night before or intend on breaking today. Unfortunately, the slice of pizza you grabbed from Mr. Z's at four in the morning isn't going to give your body the much-needed nutrients it is looking for, though vitamin-enriched pizza would be a pretty good idea. All of the dehydration has lead to extreme vitamin loss. While you are busy

"March is the month God created to show people who don't drink what hangovers are like."
~ Garrison Kellior

25

writing your phone number on the restroom stalls, your body is literally pissing away vitamins. B1, B6, B12, be whatever age you want to be, but it's time grow up enough to head to the store and load your body up with some of the nutrients it will be dropping off around town. Avoid the temptation for Flintstones and get a reputable, brand name multi-vitamin for adults, even if you don't act like one. Something like Centrum or One-A-Day should do the trick. We are big fans of the B-complex, but that may be too complex for you right now. Small reminder: Be sure to read the instructions on the bottle. It tells you how many pills to take, but you will also find great advice on what to do before you take your vitamins. Anyone feeling hungry?

Supersize Me:

Finally a book that encourages you to eat crappy food! At first we were concerned about our readers suing us when they got fat, but drinkers are easy to discredit in court and your liver will probably give out before we go to trial. Why eat crap, you ask? When your tummy is full it takes the alcohol longer to absorb. The more food in your belly, the more booze it can absorb. This means your body has more time to work on the toxins because it takes them longer to get out of the crappy food in your stomach. Fatty foods and carbohydrates do the best job, so don't hesitate to order the bacon double-cheeseburger, chocolate shake and double order of fries from the lunch counter at Dennis Pharmacy. Call it the anti-hangover special. They will have no

92% of those who consume alcohol say they've never called in sick to work because of a hangover.

idea what you are talking about, and will most likely look at you like the alcohol-saturated alien that you are, but if enough people order that way, they will be forced to acknowledge it and we will be famous for creating a new trend. As the night goes on the burger and fries will be your best friends and the chocolate shake will be like a good acquaintance. They will greet the liquor as it comes to the party in your stomach, show it around, make it feel comfortable, rub its feet, and ensure it does not leave through the same door it came in. Puking on the dance floor at Sloppy Joe's does not go over well. Trust us on this one, we speak from experience. Don't worry, eat crappy.

Prepare for the Future:

You are well rested, your belly is full and almost every letter of the alphabet is floating around your bloodstream. You've done everything you can to stop the hangover before it starts, but that doesn't mean one is not coming. It's better to be safe than sorry. Just one more chore and you will be ready to paint the town brown. Hangovers are like hurricanes; they both blow, we know they are coming, we know the damage they can cause, and we know there are certain supplies that should be kept on hand, but like the hurricanes, we assume the hangovers will miss us so we don't get supplies until it is too late. Not anymore. Put on your shopping shoes and get ready for a hurricane hangover preparedness kit that will send even the toughest hangover packing. Start in style with a dark pair of sunglasses to keep that bright

How can I be so thirsty when I drank so much last night.

light away; happy eyes - happy brain. Be sure to grab plenty of fresh spring water, a bottle of Advil, Gatorade and a bunch of bananas to keep your organs happy and on their way to recovery. Comfort foods are important, so don't hold back on the peanut M&M's, Cool Ranch Doritos or Choco Taco's, and as long as you are in the frozen food section pick up a bag of frozen peas to place on your brain when the morning comes. Mindless reading is important, so stock up on extra copies of this book or grab a "Weekly World News." It is hard to feel sorry for yourself when you discover the fattest Siamese twins in the world died when their stomachs exploded. Speaking of explosions, grab some Imodium, an extra roll of toilet paper and mouthwash. No sissy mints – you need Listerine. Last but not least, grab a six pack of beer. Drink a few before you go out and save the rest for morning. You may want to drink them when you see what you brought home with you.

And now you are prepared. Feel free to crack that first beer, but don't drink too much yet. The next section of the Key West Hangover Survival Guide contains valuable information you can use in the bars, but first let's see what we have learned so far

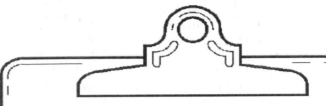

What Did We Learn?

- Alcohol does some nasty things to our bodies and hangovers are bad.

- Oreo cookies come from a gland in our brain.

- Alcohol masks our fears, lowers our inhibitions and helps us get lucky.

- Our kidneys like cookies.

- If we take a nap, pop a vitamin and eat a bunch of high carb, greasy food we will be able to stay out later and minimize our pain the following day.

- David and Chris want to create a special at Dennis Pharmacy.

- Vomiting on the floor at Sloppy Joe's will not help us get lucky.

- Frozen peas make good ice packs.

- Hurricanes and hangovers blow.

Women are significantly more likely to have a hangover after two to four drinks than men.

Some Things to Consider Before You Get Drunk

• Carry a card with the name and address of the place you are staying. Hand it to the taxi driver before you pass out in his cab.

• The meter maid wakes up earlier than you. Taxis cost less than parking tickets.

• Bring a condom. Your luck could change.

• Bring gum. Your breath stinks.

Alcohol may be the road to nowhere but at least it's a silent route.

Ask The Locals

"Mimosas in the hot tub"
~ Tim Schwartz ~ Awful Arthur's

"Spicy Clamato Mary and bustin' a nut"
~ Barbara Grob ~ Art Slut

"Lift up your shirt and lower your sweats so you look like Buddah. Get in the lotus position and sip an orange Hi-C through a big straw."
~ Grubby ~ Bagatelle

"Boiled whiskey with a drop of lemon and a drop of butter."
~ Tavito Marrero

"Best way to stop hangovers? Practice."
~ Stephanie ~ Hog's Breath Saloon

"I've been so frickin' busy I haven't had time to get a hangover."
~ Leigh Pujado ~ Louie's Backyard

roboneal.com
Jimmy Buffett doesn't know he is in our book

33

No Key West hangover guide would be complete without some sage advice from the Mayor of Margaritaville. Jimmy Buffett mastered the art of drinking in Key West and captured the island spirit of hammocks and hangovers in song. What would Jimmy do? We were too hungover to track him down and ask so we plucked these gems from his lyrics and applied them to hangovers. We know his songs by heart, let's hope we spelled them out right.

One way to get a hangover:
"I took off for a weekend last month just to try and recall the whole year. All of the faces and all of the places, wondering where they all disappeared. I didn't ponder the question too long I was hungry and went out for a bite. Ran into a chum with a bottle of rum and we wound up drinking all night."
- *Changes in Latitudes, Changes in Attitudes*

Hangover Food?
"Cheeseburger in paradise, making the best of every virtue and vice. Worth every damn bit of sacrifice to get a cheeseburger in paradise."
- *Cheeseburger in Paradise*

Suits and Fruits:
"Grapefruit. A bathing suit. You chew a little Juicy Fruit. Wash away the night. Yeah you chew a little Juicy Fruit. It's good for ya soul."
- *Grapefruit Juicy Fruit*

> Without question, the greatest invention
> in the history of mankind is beer.
> Oh, I grant you that the wheel was also a fine invention,
> but the wheel does not go nearly as well with pizza.
> ~ Dave Barry

Positive Attitude:

"I'm growing older but not up. My metabolic rate is pleasantly stuck. Let those winds of time blow over my head. I'd rather die while I'm livin' than live while I'm dead."

- I'm Growing Older but Not Up

Endurance:

"I have been drunk now for over two weeks. Passed out and I rallied and I sprung a few leaks. But I've got stop wishin', got to go fishin' I'm down to rock bottom again. Just a few friends, just a few friends."

-A Pirate Looks at Forty

Bloody Mary:

"Squalls out on the Gulf Stream. Big storm's comin' soon. I passed out in my hammock and God I slept 'til way past noon. Stood up and tried to focus. I hoped I wouldn't have to look far. I knew I could use a bloody mary. So I stumbled next door to the bar. And now I must confess, I could use some rest. I can't run at this pace very long. Yes it's quite insane. I think it hurts my brain. But it cleans me out and then I can go on."

- Tryin' to Reason With Hurricane Season

After a Night on Duval Street:

"Gotta get a little orange juice and a Darvon for my head. I can't spend all day, baby – layin' in the bed. I'm gonna go down to Fausto's get some chocolate milk. Can't spend my life in your sheets of silk. I've got to find my way. Crawl out and greet the day."

- My head hurts, my feet stink, and I don't love Jesus

rob_oneal.com
The thumb of Chris Shultz appears because it was not busy

Painting
the Town

Congratulations on making it through bootlegger's camp! You now know your enemy and are prepared to fight. There will be more rules of engagement on this bloody mary battlefield, but we will pull through and win. We are warriors, marines of the bottle, ninjas of the nightlife. Come troops, let's head to the first bar. Follow our command and don't fire until you see the whites of their wines.

Get Off Scotch Free:

There are toxins in alcohol called congeners. In order to avoid yet another scientific term, we will call them badgers. As you may know, badgers are furry little creatures that look cute from far away but the closer you get, the more dangerous they become.

There is a direct correlation between the type of alcohol you drink and the type of hangover you get. It all depends on how many badgers live in your brew of choice. Badgers like dark places, so you will find lots of badgers in red wine, whiskey, and tequila. Watch out for them in the alleyway, too. Though badgers can be found in the light, they are not as likely to gather in large groups and are easily identified by their sunglasses, so feel free to let loose on the white wine, gin and vodka. The dark side is evil, stay in the light. Your hangover will thank you tomorrow and you can irritate your friends by walking around saying, "Badgers? We don't need no stinking badgers."

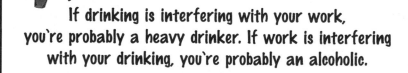

If drinking is interfering with your work, you're probably a heavy drinker. If work is interfering with your drinking, you're probably an alcoholic.

Mixed Feelings:

Few things are as tempting as chasing a beer with a shot of Jagermeister and polishing it off with a wine spritzer. Ah, the college years. The flavor combination is like an orgasm in your mouth, but you are a soldier, not a hooker. The key here is to resist the temptation to mix different types of alcohol and think about the badgers. What ever you do, don't forget the badgers. They're sneaky little bastards and they will get you when you least expect it, running out from the dark and blindsiding you with a nasty hangover. A long time ago there was a united race of badgers, strong, powerful and well organized, but eventually there was a power struggle between the three badger leaders. A huge badger war broke out and the three groups separated into wine badgers, beer badgers and liquor badgers. The three tribes of badgers hate each other with a passion and if you mix two or more types of badgers in your system they will fight each other tooth and nail until you are lying in bed wishing Satan would hurry up and claim your badger-mixing soul. Save a badger – don't mix drinks.

Women's Lib:

Hello ladies. This section is especially for you. Our apologies for the hooker comment, we meant nothing by it. Over the years, society has tried to teach women that they are equal to men in every aspect. We are all in favor of women's rights, but please do not try to match the men drink for drink in the bar. There are

plenty of women who can drink men under the table, but for the average woman out there we will reiterate, please do not try to keep up with the big, dumb, booze-hounding men you associate with. There are a bunch of chemicals with really long names that our bodies produce to help break down the toxins in alcohol. Women have fewer of these chemicals with really long names, so it takes you longer to get all the badgers out of your system. Even though you might look really cool matching the guys shot for shot, they will be out riding jet skis the next morning while you are busy proving that women can get the dry heaves too. Do you really want to prove your equality in the bathroom? Don't be afraid to turn down a shot in favor of another beer, or even a glass of water. Men are pigs and we will sleep with you anyway. And speaking of men, there is another "M" word we should all get to know.

The 'M' Word:

It is not a politically correct term and should only be brought up with caution in Key West. Some people use the word freely in close circles, but they are the ones who end up looking stupid. We will use the term here for educational purposes, but after reading this chapter it shall never be uttered again. "Moderation."

There, we said it. Please don't tell anyone. We have our reputations to consider. Let's break down what moderation is all about and what it means to you and your hangover. It takes your

"I think a man ought to get drunk at least twice a year just on principle, so he won't let himself get snotty about it."
~ Raymond Chandler

body about an hour to process one drink. This would make one drink an hour an ideal night out for your body, but leaves you with the problem of what to do for the remaining 56 minutes between drinks. Moderation is tricky, but you can try to distract yourself from drinking by engaging in activities such as billiards, darts, perusing the jukebox selection, smoking pot or having sex in the bathroom. You could even try crazy concepts such as drinking slower. We know moderation is not always a popular choice, but it will lessen your hangover and it beats the hell out of abstinence. If you are the type of person who always needs a beverage in your hand, there are other options.

Water World:

How many times must you be told to drink a glass of water after each alcoholic drink? 8,009,008 since 1996, at least. Though water may not have fancy commercials with girls in bikinis and giant horses, H_2O does have some benefits. In addition to being free, water will also dilute the nasty badgers and momentarily call off the Oreo strike thus helping to hold off dehydration. If you are concerned about your friends giving you a hard time, add a lime to your water and drink it from a rocks glass. You'll look classy, and will have the last laugh the next morning you as they beg for a sip of your Evian. Twenty bucks is the going rate before noon.

ARGGH MATIES!
Don't Drink and Drive!
305-295-0000

Top Shelf:

Good booze costs more because it has less crap in it. Just as a Lexus looks nicer, handles better and provides a smoother ride than, say, a 1986 Chevette, top shelf liquor tastes nicer, handles better and provides a smoother hangover. Lexus and top shelf both cost more, but you get what you pay for. Better booze is simply much nicer to drive. If you are going to take a walk down liquor lane, spend the extra bucks and go with something other than the house. Never go for the bottle that simply says "VODKA." Step it up a notch and grab some Stoli, Grey Goose or Van Gogh. This is another one of those times when illogical reasoning sets in. You refuse to splurge an extra two dollars for a Stoli, Grey Goose or Van Gogh, but buying a round of shots for the bachelor or bachelorette party is no problemo. The problem here is that the liquor is going home with you while the bachelor or bachelorette party is not. Upgrading to top shelf liquor: $2. Round of shots for the wedding party: $56. Waking up alone without a hangover...priceless.

Up in Smoke:

Smoking and drinking go together like chocolate and peanut butter. Both are pretty good by themselves, but mixed together they create a sensation. Just ask E.T. The major difference would be that the smell of peanut butter in your hair doesn't make you want to vomit after a heavy night of hitting the chocolate. In case you haven't been listening to the surgeon general, smoking is bad for you. Sure, cigarettes taste yummy, look cool and make

**Learn to appreciate hangovers.
If it was all good times every jackass would be doing it.**

you feel like Betty Davis or Cary Grant. What else would you expect for $7 but 20 beautiful moments in an easy-to-carry package? Unfortunately, all the nasty stuff in those 20 beautiful moments comes back to haunt you the next day. It all boils down to just how many toxins your body can handle. One at a time is usually a good rule of thumb, so let's stick with drinking for now. You will have a much better chance of getting your peanut butter in someone else's chocolate.

Know When to Say When:

Many of us are powerless when it comes to leaving a bar by our own free will and choose to rely on last call, a nagging spouse or the local sheriff. It would be wasteful to leave with all of that booze on the shelf. Thankfully, bars stay open late in Key West and when 2 a.m. rolls around you will be more concerned with creating dirty lyrics to accompany "Money Money" than thinking about your impending hangover. The bars will remain open for two solid hours, but these are the danger hours, Will Robinson. The decisions you make during these two hours will greatly affect the intensity of your hangover. By 2 a.m. nearly everyone is trashed, three sheets to wind, wrecked and drunk as a skunk. A benefit of this is that no one will notice what, if or how much you are drinking. Drunk people are relatively easy to confuse. You may be pretty drunk at this point yourself, but if you are going to stay out for the next two hours, switch to water! Water is your friend. Two hours of drinking water instead of booze will benefit you so much the next day you are likely to call us with an invite for

A hangover is a wrath of grapes.

Bloody Marys. You will feel a million times better in the morning, save money, and lessen your chances of getting arrested. Another bonus: Everyone around you will be so hammered it will be hard to resist the opportunity to take advantage of drunk people and you will be the smoothest dancer in the bar. Evian, please.

Your Mama Don't Dance and Your Daddy Don't Rock 'n' Roll:

Have a couple of cocktails and the dance floor starts looking pretty good. Busta Moves is in da house and before long you are busting moves all over the place, doing the worm across the bar and busting your ankle. Apart from the broken limbs and public humiliation that often accompany drunk dancing, your John Travolta imitation is also helping your hangover win the war. It may be fun, and you look really cool, but unfortunately dancing, or any physical activity for that matter, increases your heart rate. This makes blood circulate faster delivering more alcohol at a quicker rate and causing a badger traffic jam at your liver. Badgers hate traffic jams. You are also expending precious energy the body will need as it tries to repair itself from all of the damage the alcohol is doing. All of this jiggling around may make you break a sweat, so now you are depleting minerals and speeding dehydration. All of this adds up to a hellacious hangover. We're not saying you have to stay off the dance floor and keep your sweet moves to yourself. Just use them in moderation and don't make a night out of it. Who wants to be the sweaty dance machine anyway?

ISLAND JOE'S COFFEE SAYS:
If the morning is a little fuzzy and you need a pick me up try Misty Mornings. Enjoy reminiscing about last night's good times or planning future ones. This is a wonderful light to medium roast with an exotic aroma guaranteed to get you ready to find another good time.

IslandJoesGourmetCoffee.com

The ring finger of Chris Shultz does not appear because it was busy

No animals got drunk in the making of this picture

Are You
Being a
Drunken
Ass?

Are you making a drunken ass of yourself?
Take the quiz and find out for sure.

1. **How many drinks have you spilled tonight?**
   a. None
   b. One, but a drunk guy bumped into me.
   c. Juz a cubble. Hey, itsh Key Wesht!
   d. I didn't kill any chinks.
   e. Circle e if you can not read this.

2. **Which best describes the bartender's attitude towards you?**
   a. Prompt, friendly service. They bought me the last round.
   b. The drinks are a bit weak, but so are my tips.
   c. It took me fifteen minutes to get this drink. What a joke.
   d. Whaat bartendra? Ohhh, shcrew hurr. Sheesha bitcsh.

3. **How are things going with members of the opposite sex tonight?**
   a. I'm still working up the courage to approach them.
   b. Is there a sign on my back that says "Talk to me if you are drunk?"
   c. Everyone in this bar is a stuck-up looser.
   d. I sthink zha bartendra wunz ta shleep with me.

---

4. Which of the following is most likely to bring out your violent side?
    a. I don't like violence.
    b. A man beating up on a woman.
    c. That dude better stop looking at me!
    d. Zshat metal pole isha shtupid bitcsh. I'm shorry, I lub yoo, maan.

5. Key West is the perfect place to:
    a. Kick back and catch a tan.
    b. Waste away in Margaritaville.
    c. Get Duval faced on shit street.
    d. Whersh ma schooter? Em gonna kick zhat gay guyzch assh.

6. The Key West police are:
    a. Here to protect and serve
    b. They won't bother me as long as I keep myself in line
    c. Fun to wrestle with.
    d. Hesh lucky theesh hamcufshs ar on ori'd wip hish asshh!

"Sometimes when I reflect back on all the beer I drank I feel ashamed. Then I look Into the glass and think about the workers in the brewery and all of their hopes and dreams. If I didn't drink this beer they might be out of work and their dreams would be shattered. Then I say to myself, it is better that I drink this beer and let their dreams come true than be selfish and worry about my liver."
~ Jack Handy

WE HAVE THE ANSWERS!
How did you score?

Mostly A: You are a little tame for Key West, but relatively harmless. You are definitely not making a drunken ass of yourself, but there is probably something goofy about your outfit.

Mostly B: Congrats. You are not a drunken ass, but you might be a liar. We like you anyway. Stick around for a while... the next round is on us. Start tipping your bartender better and you'll be loved even more.

Mostly C: You probably don't realize it yet, but you are a drunken ass. As the alcohol continues to pulse through your veins your condition will worsen. Don't be offended when people compare you to a hemorrhoid.

Mostly D: You are not a drunken ass. You are a drunken asshole. Do us all a favor by extinguishing your flame and getting the hell out of Key West. The tribe has spoken.

More signs you are making an ass of yourself:
• You are the only one on the dance floor and no music
  is playing.
• Homeless people don't ask you for change.
• Dogs cross the street as you approach them.
• Your jokes seem funnier than the guy on stage.
• Destruction of personal property seems like a good idea.
• You are not wearing pants.
• There is an object on your head other than a hat or
  bandanna.

Ask The Locals

"Three words that don't have much meaning
in Key West: Normal, time, hangover."
~ Joe Forte, Artist

"I'm a dumb blonde and I don't know anything
about drinking or hangovers...
Where is Key West?"
~ Kenna Pancamo

"The feather of the chicken that bit you is the
best way to get rid of hangover."
~ Helen O'Connel, Grand Vin

"Key West sunsets are better than sunrises.
Especially if you are hungover."
~ Tim Hammontree

"If you sleep long enough you don't get hungover."
~ Keith St. Peter

"Soaking my feet in a warm tub of butter."
~ Stock Island Boy, Meteor Smokehouse

"Mimosas and a pedicure."
~ Jodi Bombace

roboneal.com
Beautiful woman on taxi: Jaime Montgomery
Coolest taxi driver in town: Skip Hurst

So you made it to last call and you're still walking in a fairly straight line, ready for more? Alas, the night is over and you have no choice but to get some sleep or watch "Law and Order" reruns on TNT. Not so fast there, drunkie. You are engaged in a war of attrition with a Key West hangover and it will stop at nothing to keep you out. No street is an easy passage and even the cabbies can be dangerous. No place is safe until your mind shuts your body down and you head off to sleepy land. Your journey home will be filled with drunken distractions attempting to keep you away from the safety of your own bed. Temptation will be your escort. Be aware of your enemies and you will go on to drink another day. The following is a breakdown of the many dangers you will face after last call.

Lock-ins:

If a bar closes at 4 a.m., does it really mean the bar is closed? This is not one of those "tree in the forest" SAT questions, so don't think too hard. Spend some time in Key West and you will realize that every morning around 3:58 a.m. the bouncers and bartenders protect their establishment's liquor license by telling everyone to follow the rest of the cattle and get the hell out. "You don't have to go home, but you can't stay here." This technique may seem a bit harsh, but they are professionals and there is no time to debate liquor laws with intoxicated law students. These servers are ready to sit down and have a tasty beverage of their own as they count their hard-earned tips, but special people may

"I feel sorry for people who don't drink.
When they wake up in the morning,
that's as good as they're going to feel all day."
~ Frank Sinatra

be allowed to stay behind. If you rode on the short bus, this does not mean you, but if you are good friends with the bartender you may make the cut. It is not unusual for the bartender to kick back a few brews with his friends behind closed doors, and if there are several employees with several special friends, the doors are locked, the windows are covered, bottles start opening and it becomes what is known as a lock-in. Don't go asking bartenders if you can "stay for the lock-in." You will look like a jackass and they don't want you there. Some bars have lock-ins, some do not. Why are we telling you this? On the off chance that the bartenders like you and invite you to stick around for a beer, we don't want you to be shocked and act like a jackass. You should also know that this invite means heavy drinking 'til sunrise and a one-way trip to hangover hell on the short bus. Wear a helmet.

After-Hours:

A true drinker won't let something as minor as the bars closing stop them from getting a drink. There are houses with liquor cabinets, speakeasy bars and stocked hotel rooms just calling out for a party in the great, wide world of Key West after hours. These parties, held between the hours of 4 a.m. and the cops arriving are called after-hours. There is a great history of after hours in Key West. Beyond the Heaven and Hell party, some of our personal favorites were known as Shady Acres, and Hula's. These spot have long since died, but the crack-of-dawn clubs continue and the memories are legendary.

Where are they now? We're not putting them in print. If the regular spots are not open or simply shut down, new locations are decided shortly after last call. In a larger city these parties would not be such a problem, but in Key West word travels quickly through the coconut telegraph. Before you know it, half of Old Town is crammed into a small house and the police are banging on the door. People are inspired to drink fast and hard, but these extra hours of hard core pounding will result in a pounding head when you come to that afternoon. If you do not know where a party is, walk down any street in Old Town and look for the noisy house. Some of these parties are private, but with many you can just walk in, tell them you are supposed to meet David and Chris, and act like you belong. If it is obvious you are not welcome say, "wrong house," and leave. None of this will help your hangover, but it will have a lot of people wondering who David and Chris are.

Drugs:

If you smell pot wafting through the air on your way home, pay no attention to the voice in your head telling you to make friends with the people smoking it. Same goes for the guy selling crack, or the chick shooting heroin behind the abandoned building. We all love to mix drugs and alcohol once in a blue moon, and those little bumps in the road keep you moving, but unfortunately these drugs mimic alcohol by keeping Oreos away from different organs and unleashing badgers in an incredible war. Drug badg-

ers warring booze badgers creates a volatile situation that ends in a hellacious hangover that can only be remedied by a day or two in bed. Though pot in the morning may make your hangover easier to deal with and makes bad movies funnier, marijuana is illegal and nothing is worse than a hangover in jail. Say no to drugs... and stay in school.

Fights:

There is one thing worse than a hangover in jail: A hangover in the hospital with three cracked ribs, a broken jaw and an imprint of a Corona bottle on your forehead. The right mix of alcohol has a knack for bringing out the WWF wrestler in all of us, and while you may be perfectly happy taking out your rage on inanimate objects, there are people out there who won't think twice about giving you a smack down on Caroline Street simply because you were walking on the wrong side of the road and their mother never gave them enough hugs as a child. Drunks and fights go hand in hand and you don't need any help making your head throb in pain come breakfast time. Your chances of getting lucky may increase, but your hangover will be in full force and they do not serve Gatorade. The view from the cells overlooking the ocean is breathtaking, but jail is jail and it is a long walk home from Stock Island the next day. Help your hangover and make it home without seeing the bars from the inside.

**Time is never wasted
if you're wasted all the time.**

Booze at home:

We never saw the movie, but if "The Last Temptation of Christ" took place in Key West, the last temptation was probably the booze stash back at the manger. Luckily, the citizens of Key West do not have the powers of Jesus or the entire Gulf of Mexico would be a fine cabernet and the Atlantic a pinot noir. When you finally get home and open the fridge after your crazy night on the town, resist all temptations to drink more booze. There is still plenty left in your bloodstream and it has done its job for the night. More won't help you sleep; it won't make you feel better in the morning; it won't help you get lucky and you will probably pass out before you take your first sip. You are trying to fight off a tremendous hangover, so don't just go flopping yourself into the bed yet, either. There is still work to be done if you don't want to wake up feeling like Frank Sinatra's liver.

Water You Talkin' Bout?

Going down a water slide is much less painful when you have plenty of water. The same could be said for a hangover, except you run less of a risk of getting caught in the plastic tunnel. Remember we told you to put that bottle of wine down before you went to bed? Now is the time to help yourself out and get some proper hydration. Water will help get the Oreo factory back in production and slow down the battling badgers. We've said it before and we will say it again. Drink a big bottle of water before you go to bed! It will not be a pleasant task, but you will feel bet-

ter in the morning. Trust us. It is late, you are tired. We won't go into the how and why right now, but pretend you are Nike and just do it!

Pain in the aspirin:

As long as you are chugging water, pop a couple of Advil. They're not just for periods anymore. Not only will it help with your headache, but it also gets rid of the water weight gain from all of the H2O you are drinking.

I'm a Seven...

Urinate! Potty humor aside, go to the bathroom. Seriously, we mean it. Take an extra minute to visit the bathroom before you go to sleep. Don't worry about waking anyone up, you have done that already, and taking a pee before you go to bed will dump out more of those nasty toxins. You rid yourself of the vitamins about fourteen cocktails ago, and taking a leak before you go to bed will mean one less trip to the loo in the middle of the night, hence a better rest. It will also lessen your chances of wetting the bed. If you can find the energy, brush your teeth too. You stink like booze and the bad breath bacteria are starting to multiply. Avoid the temptation to clean your teeth and pee at the same time or your tooth brush could become the toilet brush and leave a bad taste in your mouth. Don't forget to wipe the seat.

Get Naked:

You have been trying to take off your clothes all night long, so don't let the lack of spectators stop you now. It is always tempting to sleep in your shoes, pants and goofy shirt, but after a hard night battling the booze the effort can be too much and climbing under the covers is simply out of the question. Making the most of your remaining sleep time is crucial. Sleeping in your clothes can cut off circulation, leave funny button marks on your body, and increase the risk of back pains associated with sleeping on your wallet or purse. Ever smell your clothes after a night at the bar? It brings back fond memories of spilled margaritas, cigarettes, late night pizza and dance floor sweat, none of which will benefit you in the morning. In this situation it's best to simply get naked, take some pictures with your camera phone and send them to info@phantompress.com. Now make the effort to climb under those soft covers and your job is done.

Beer is the cause of and solution
to all of life's problems.
~Homer Simpson

What Did We Learn?

- There are drinking opportunities after the bars close.

- People don't want you at their lock-in.

- People don't want you at their after hours, but you might be able to stay by dropping Chris' and David's names.

- Don't smoke crack.

- Fights are better when viewed from a taxi.

- Holograms will shoot from our heads in the future.

- The jail is your best option for getting laid.

- Frank Sinatra is dead but his music lives on.

- Send naked pictures.

WHAT ISLAND JOE DRINKS TO GET GOING.
2 shots of V8 juice, one shot of Black Flag Espresso with 2 tablespoons of ginger to settle the stomach, salt and pepper.

IslandJoesGourmetCoffee.com

Ziggy's Devil appears courtesy of the Chicken Store

roboneal.com

The
Morning
After

The Morning After

Good morning, er...afternoon, sleepy head! The time of day is not important, and although you probably feel like attending your own funeral, we are pleased to inform you that the attempted suicide last night was not a success. Right now you are not thinking straight. If you listened to us at all thus far, you're naked, under the covers, not beat up or in jail and you have naked pictures of yourself on your cell phone. You also have a complete hangover kit prepared for this dire situation. The first decisions you make when you wake up with a hangover are also the most crucial. Chris and David, your hangover heroes, are here to help, and apart from the pictures, we have not steered you wrong yet.Ignore the voice in your head urging you to, "crawl in hole and die," and listen to your hangover specialists. We are here to save the day.

Attitude Adjustment:

Stop feeling sorry for yourself. Your glass may have been overflowing last night, but that is no excuse to take the "glass half empty approach" now. Feel lousy? So do the other 18,000 people in Key West who managed to make it from sunset to last call, but they are making the most of this beautiful day. There are people with headaches enjoying their pain at the Southernmost Pool; those with stomach aches taking in sites while vomiting off the back of a Conch Train; folks in bath towels wandering the streets

of Key West looking for their hotel wondering what the hell happened to their clothes. There are also people living in Key West who had to work this morning. They called in sick hours ago and are getting a nice tan at the beach, but look at you. Lying in bed looking smug is no way to deal with a Key West hangover. You are a soldier and it is time to get up and act like one.

Here is some motivation to get you on your feet:

- This is Key West. You can stay in bed anywhere.
- The ham and cheese omelet won't come to you.
- The longer you stay in bed, the nastier your sheets will get.
- If you let your significant other out alone they will cheat on you.
- Jimmy Buffett is in town.
- The bars are open.

Water (Part 1)

We hope you are into role-playing. This is a scene from the old claymation "Rudolph the Red Nosed Reindeer" and you get to be the Abominable Snowman. If at all possible, find some volunteers to play Herbie, the elf who wants to be a dentist, and Yukon Cornelius, the bearded explorer. Now, locate the nearest bottle of water and sing: "Put one foot in front of the other and soon you'll be walking cross the floor. Put one foot in front of the other and soon you'll be walking out the door. Put one foot in front of

Even though a number of people have tried,
no one has yet found a way
to drink for a living.
~Jean Kerr

the other and soon you'll be able to drink some more." Keep singing the song in your head as you drink the water, but resist the urge to act like a ventriloquist. Feel free to make up your own verses as you head to the bathroom. There are eighteen words that rhyme with floor and you will need them all. The water you just drank will start fighting dehydration and ease the dryness in your mouth as well as the pounding in your head. Bring the bottle in the bathroom and drink it while you pee. It's called multitasking.

Bloody Mary Time

Turn off the bathroom light, and put your face right up to the mirror. Now stare in to the mirror and say "Bloody Mary" thirteen times. This will do nothing to cure your hangover, but according to Brian, our third-grade camp counselor, it will cause the evil spirit of a ghost named Mary to come out of the mirror and claw your eyes. We were too frightened to try this ourselves, so if you make it out alive be sure to let us know how it works. Now stop staring at the mirror, drink some more water and close the bathroom door. We have some business to take care of.

Taking Care of Business

Your body is full of toxins and this is no time to be bathroom shy. Romantic getaway be damned, it is time for you to do your business. Drop the kids off at the pool, go number two, drop a deuce, poop, call it what you want – just get it done. This can be

a noisy experience, depending on how much of what you drank last night, so don't hesitate to turn the shower on in advance. If there is a radio crank it up and if there are any innocent bystanders around, try sending them to the store for some Advil or a newspaper. Don't forget to flush. Now let's hit the showers.

Shower Power

Why should you shower? Because you stink like a cigarette that was extinguished in a puddle of sweat, drool and vomit, and the water is free. Showers have several benefits when it comes to a hangover. In addition to masking your bathroom sounds, the pulsing water will ease tension in your muscles, releasing built-up toxins and helping those aches and pains. This is a good day to start using wash cloths because your pores are clogged with junk. Imagine the badgers hanging out in your body getting fat and then trying to climb out of tiny little holes. They get stuck, and the only way to get them out is to chop off their heads with a warm soapy wash cloth. Soap your body twice because you are going to miss some spots. When it comes to shampoo, wash, rinse and repeat. Resist the urge to sit down in the tub while the shower is running, especially if you just peed. This is not a bubble bath and we will not have you treating it like one. You have other things to take care of to cure this hangover. Now, grab a towel that has not yet been used to clean up a spill or vomit and head back to the mirror. You look a dozen times better, those bags under your eyes are fading away, the cigarette stench is

Finish your beer,
there are sober people in China.

gone and you are starting to resemble a human being. You clean up pretty nice, but let's do something about your breath.

Cavity Creeps

Your mouth contains more organisms than a Petri dish, but that won't stop us from kissing you. Others may feel differently, so it is time to brush your teeth. Four out of five dentists recommend toothpaste for people who want to attract the opposite sex. The fifth dentist is gay and recommends it for people who want to attract the same sex. Small up and down strokes are the key to success, working it all around so you hit the right spots. Doesn't that feel good? This brushing technique will leave your mouth feeling wintry fresh and satisfied. You should gargle with Listerine, holding it in your mouth as long as you can and being careful not to swallow. No need to floss today – like you were going to anyway.

Don't Sweat It

Time is ticking away so you can forget your daily bathroom rituals involving cologne, perfume, make-up, nail polish and small animal sacrifices. Your poor pores are trying to hasten your recovery by sweating out those nasty badgers. It looks like a sweaty day, so put on some deodorant to mask the scent of chocolate martini escaping from your pores and leave it at that. If you are a particularly ugly creature we will permit a little eye shadow. Save the shaving for later; your skin is puffy, your hands are shaking and are not yet capable of handling sharp objects.

"Alcohol may be man's worst enemy, but the bible says love your enemy."
~ Frank Sinatra

Water (Part 2)

Drink another bottle of water. Your body needs it to wash out a fresh bunch of nasty badgers and you sound sophisticated saying "Aquafina." The water will also help you wash down the pills you are about to swallow. Don't worry we're not talking about those kind of pills... junkie.

Pain Relievers

There is risk involved with taking pain relievers after drinking alcohol, but you are probably not concerned about your liver if your head is performing the Broadway version of "The Telltale Heart." Acetaminophen is not your friend this morning. It may help your head, but combined with alcohol it is virtually putting your liver through the blender. Read the labels on your pain reliever and stay away from the Tylenol. Avoid pills that contain caffeine as well. Aspirin will do a good job combating the swelling in your head, but it can be tough on your stomach. This can lead to a bleeding tummy, vomiting or both. Ibuprofen may be your best bet, but researchers determined to make us suffer have found it may make our stomachs bleed as well. If you want to play it safe, take two M&Ms and call us in the morning.

Dress for Less

Tight jeans and a push-up bra might attract the attention you never received from your father, but attention is the last thing you need right now. Circulation is an important factor in living,

69

especially when you feel like you are going to die. Throw on a loose-fitting pair of shorts and a baggy t-shirt and leave the bra behind. That goes for you too, girls. Comfort is the theme for today and your personal comfort is far more important than the guy in the restaurant urging his pal to turn around and check out the rack on the chick with no bra. Sorry for talking to the ladies on that one guys, but we all mastered the art of dressing like we just don't care a long time ago.

Water (Part 3)

Drink more water. Do not walk out that door without a bottle of water. It may be hot, you will be thirsty, and the 37 minutes it takes to get a piece of bacon in your mouth will seem like 37 hours. Treat the water like it is your daughter, and never leave without it.

Things Remembered

We realize your mind is still fragile. Here are some items you might want to bring along as we enter the second phase of recovery:

- A hat to block the sun. Lotion clogs your pores.
- Money for impulse buys and food.
- Vitamins, but don't take them yet.
- I.D. You will be drinking again soon.
- A key for each member of your party. The ones who did not read this might not make it through the day.
- Sunglasses. The sun is much closer to the earth today.
- This book. Your recommendation could buy our next drink.

What Did We Learn?

- My glass feels half empty but is really half full.
- The locals called in sick and poor service is to be expected.
- I get to be the Abominable Snowman!
- David and Chris have a water fetish.
- There is an evil spirit in my mirror.
- Other people suffer from poopophobia.
- Sitting down in the shower is lazy.
- Some dentists are gay.
- I use too much product.
- Pain pills feel good even though they are bad.
- I dress like I do because of my dad.
- The sun is bright.
- Word of mouth will encourage others to buy this book.

Tennessee mug appears courtesy of Sarah Thomas

Hangover Cures from Around the World

Hangover cures have been around since...well, since there were hangovers. Different parts of the world have created various cures using what they had available and seemed to work best. Our crack research team found the best cures in the history of hangovers. Try these out for yourself if you have the courage.

Sweating To the Oldies.

said that American Indian tribes would run until they broke out in a sweat. They would then take a seat, lick their sweat and spit it out to rid their bodies of the poison. Our friend Marrero likes to do this every Sunday. He's not an American Indian but he does enjoy licking his own sweat and he very rarely has a hangover. Proof enough for us.

Eel Anyone?

Hangover heroes in the Middle Ages would down a plate of dried eel mixed with bitter almonds to cure their hangovers. It is said that the eel would revive itself in the stomach and drink the remaining booze, sucking the hangover away. Okay, that's a lie but the eel worked.

The Voodoo You Do

Haitian voodoo people find that the best way to get rid of a hangover is by sticking thirteen black pins in the cork of the offending bottle. This supposedly lets the sprit of the booze free, releasing it from your body and relieving your hangover.

Never underestimate the power intoxicated people in large groups.

 **Lemon**

In Puerto Rico, the most popular hangover cure is to rub half a lemon under your "drinking arm." This is the arm you most use to lift alcoholic beverages to your lips. Warning: You might not want to do this after shaving, as it could sting. Unless, of course, you're into that sort of thing.

 Chim Chimeny Chim Chimeny...

In 19th Century Merry ol' England, chimney sweeps swore by the healing properties of a long, lukewarm, soot milkshake. We have heard it also gives you the desire to sing and dance across rooftops and pick up nannyies.

 Wild West Hare Doo.

In the Wild Wild West, whisky-swilling cowboys swore by a stiff cup of rabbit-poo tea. As if morning breath wasn't bad enough already.

 Eye Eye Eye

In Outer Mongolia, drinkers suck down pickled sheep's eyeballs in tomato juice to get rid of their hangovers. In Inner Mongolia they skip the eyes and go straight for the balls.

> "There are better things in life than alcohol, but alcohol makes up for not having them."
> ~ Terry Pratchett

Not Mary Ann...Ginger!

One of the the greatest cures for nausea is drinking ginger, and it has been used by sailors to cure seasickness for hundreds of years. Crush up some ginger, add orange juice to take away the sting and chug it down. It might burn but it will do the trick.

Drink Your Veggies.

V8 is said to have more vegetables in one can that an entire field in Iowa. Yes, it tastes like crap but it does the trick, according to anybody who has tried it. Grandma loves it and she drinks a lot.

Bananas Rule.

Some guy from Ireland says, "Eat a banana as they contain potassium, which is guaranteed to revitalize your body after a heavy session." We love the Irish and they should know what cures the hangover.

Toss The Roman Salad.

The Romans ate cabbage leaves to cure their hangovers. Word on the street is they also ate fried canaries on a stick! This has evolved to our greasy fried breakfasts at diners.

Russian Vegetables.

Russians swear by sliced cucumbers to get rid of their morning-after shivers.

 Whatever Works.

Some people swear by carrot juice or milk thistle – a homeopathic remedy in capsule form.

 Germanic Ways.

German drinkers get rid of their pain with a breakfast of herrings with mustard. Good for the breath. Scares the booze away.

 Turkish Times.

Turks swear by yogurt and garlic. Hold the turkey.

"I have taken more out of alcohol
than alcohol has taken out of me."
~Winston Churchill

Ask The Locals

"Bong hit and a Gatorade."
~ Valerie, Chart Room

"I kind of feel like you should just pay for it."
~ David Litrun, Marathon Key

"Waking up and getting spanked with a large wooden spoon always does it for me."
~ Jimmy Villegas, Bartender extrordinaire

"The Red Eye Express - cheap beer and Clamato. Take the Red Eye Express back to dreamland. When you wake up have a Pepsi with chocolate milk."
~ Rick Dostal, Mojo Working Charters

"Alka Seltzer Morning and that good ol' Mountain Dew"
~ Citizen's Voice

"Since I am hungover at this particular moment, nothing comes to mind." ~
~ Niki, Hog's Breath Saloon

"French fries dipped in a chocolate milkshake and a lap dance."
~ Jeff Palmer, patron at Schooner Wharf Bar

Ask The Locals

"Drink More!"
~ Joe Wells

"Key West hangovers are great!
You just sweat it out!"
~ Jane Schultz

"Isn't that what cocaine is for?"
~ Anonymous

""If you're in Key West you don't quit drinking.
If you don't quit drinking you don't
get a hangover."
~ Dan McConnel, Flamingo Crossing

"It's always a surprise when you arrive to
work without a hangover."
~ Robin Bartley

"People can't resist my hand-job drinks."
~ Ramey, Rick's Tree Bar

"Play Baba O'Riley (Teenage Wasteland) at
full volume and jump in the Atlantic Ocean."
~Nate, Captain Tony's Saloon

We would like to take a moment to praise you for a job well done. Making it out the door is a giant first step and we were only kidding about your glass being half full. Suffering a Key West hangover is no easy task and we would applaud you, but the noise hurts your head and it is difficult to clap in a book. The worst part of your day is over and it is time to seek a reward for all of your hard work. Select a restaurant from the guide at the end of the book and let's hit the road.

The Walk of Life

You may be feeling a little better, but that is no excuse to drive a car, operate a bicycle or handle anything else with wheels.. Your reaction time is still less than desirable and hitting a dog or a parked car will only postpone nourishment and make you lose your appetite. Grabbing a cab seems logical, but a leisurely stroll is what you really need. It will provide fresh air, get your blood flowing to remove toxins, and give you a healthy excuse to eat like an overgrown pig.

Hair of the Dog?

Drinking more booze to kill your hangover is generally not a good idea. We strongly suggest that you wait until after breakfast to start boozing again, but it is your body, so do as you wish. Drinking actually will make you feel better, but you will eventually have to sober up and your hangover gets progressively worse

A hangover is something to fill a head
that was empty the night before.

.he longer you put it off. If you are going to drink immediately, or have already started, do yourself a favor and get some food in your system. A drink with breakfast instead of before breakfast is a good balance.

Pig Out?

Some scientists say that greasy food will upset your stomach and make your hangover worse. Cameron Diaz said, "Grease is the only cure for a hangover." Cameron Diaz is famous, attractive and we like how she dances in her underwear, so you should order extra bacon, double meat, onion rings and a side of sausage gravy. Imagine Cameron shaking her bacon for added flavor.

Egging You On

Eggs are a good source of protein, but what would you expect from an underdeveloped chicken? They also contain cysteine which has nothing to do with cysts but helps with toxin patrol. Eggs also taste good with cheese and add a color to your plate that makes the bacon look even more appealing, so help control our chicken population and eat some eggs.

Another Toast

By this time you should be an expert at making toasts, but we will leave this order to the cooks. Burnt toast is an excellent way to help your hangover. Cooking bread turns it into toast, but

"My mouth tastes like vomit and I don't remember a thing."
~ Ned Flanders

cooking toast turns it into carbon. Carbon is like a humane badger trap, so eating burnt toast will lock all of your badgers in solitary confinement until they are ready to die. Hospitals pump carbon into patients with alcohol poisoning so they can live to drink another day and it is also a key ingredient in some over-the-counter hangover remedies. Dr. Atkins may not approve of this cure, but the doctor is dead so eat your bread. Cheers!

Banana Split

Bananas have so many purposes. They make great telephones, remind you of monkeys, fit easily in your front pocket and help cure hangovers. Drinking is a good way to deplete your potassium supplies and bananas are a good way to replenish them. Potassium helps your nerve and muscle functions, so eat a banana and you won't twitch so much. Banana splits are highly recommended. Your body could probably use some sugar that was not derived from alcohol and ice cream will make you happy.

Juan Valdez – Friend or Foe?

Telling a caffeine addict not to drink coffee would have the effectiveness of instructing a dog not to lick his walnuts. Caffeine has some advantages and disadvantages, the down side being the diuretic effect which causes dehydration. On the up side, caffeine is a stimulant and provides a limited energy boost while reducing the size of blood vessels and helping the headache. If you don't drink coffee, don't start now. Can't live without it?

Match it with a glass of water. The same formula for booze goes with coffee.

Let Loose the Juice

Order some juice and demand that it be served in a regular sized glass. The small glasses may work for midgets, but you are a big human with a big hangover so only extra large will do. Juice is good for your hangover because it has sugar to give you energy. It also has vitamins and minerals to replace the ones you destroyed last night. If your stomach is feeling queasy, stick with water. Juice also contains some acids and you don't want to be burping up grapefruit juice at the beach. It smells weird.

Part of This Complete Breakfast

Save that last sip of water. Now grab the multivitamin from your pocket, scrape off the lint and swallow it down. (The vitamin, not the lint. Save your lint to donate to our Biggest Ball of Lint in The World!) Vitamins do more than you realize and they really work. It is important to take them with food. Nobody likes vitamins, your body included, so you must mix them with food to trick your body the same way you would give a pill to your dog. Your body will be so busy admiring the chewed-up piece of bacon it will have no idea what hit it when dosed with Bs, Cs and Ds.

Alcohol may cause you to take twice as long to recover from a good time as it did to have it.

One Last Tip

Key West is an island of adventure and we are not going to let this day get the best of us. You are probably not feeling 100% right now, so let us remind you that you may be grumpy, moody and forgetful. Your waiter or waitress was probably partying last night but still took the time to wait on your sorry ass. Don't forget to tip.

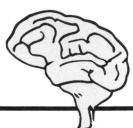

"All right, brain, I don't like you and you don't like me –
so let's just do this and I'll get back to
killing you with alcohol."
~ Homer Simpson.

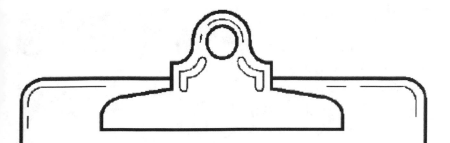

What Did We Learn?

- My glass is half empty.
- Walking justifies gluttony.
- I can drink more booze if I choose.
- Cameron Diaz likes grease.
- The egg came first.
- Dr. Atkins is dead.
- Bananas can be used as phones.
- Coffee is both good and evil.
- Grapefruit burps are strictly evil.
- My body prefers bacon to vitamins.
- Waitstaff with hangovers need tips too.

We have often been told that life is not fair, but nothing drives that point home like a Key West hangover. A night that begins with tropical breezes, laid-back attitudes and ice cold margaritas should never end with a throbbing brain, dry heaves and a foggy memory. Unfortunately for us, that is often the case.

Alcohol is bad for you, but the same can be said for fried chicken, carbohydrates, meat, milk and sticking your tongue in a fan. Red M&Ms cause cancer, standing in front of a microwave will make you impotent, pop rocks and Pepsi killed Mikey and you will go to hell if you do not accept Jesus Christ as your personal savior. The fine line between fact and fiction is increasingly harder to define as our geeky scientists and fear-based marketing companies combine the results of their various studies and unleash them on the public. At this point they take on a life of their own.

People used to die of natural causes but that is virtually non-existent these days. Something is to blame for everything, and though many drinkers never drive drunk and wreck their cars, wind up homeless on the streets or die at an early age from cirrhosis of the liver, there is an element of our nation that would like to return to the days of Prohibition. Frank Purcell once said, "I'll support the rights of smokers until I die, because as soon as they get them, they are coming after the drinkers." Twenty years later the smokers are being driven towards extinction. If history does indeed repeat itself, the return of Prohibition may not be far away.

Moderation seems to be a rule of the universe. Don't do too much of anything and you will be okay. Vacations also seem to be a rule of the universe, and they are the perfect opportunity to overindulge. With over three million people visiting Key West every year, there is going to be some heavy drinking, and with that comes some heavy hangovers. While we would hope you don't drink too much, that is usually not the case.

We hope this book has given you more insight into your hangover than you ever wished to have. Though you probably paid no attention to the tips for avoiding or preventing a hangover before and during your drinking escapades, perhaps some of it will stick with you the next time you go on a bender. Maybe you thought the book was a bunch of crap, but if it took your mind off the pounding in your skull, or passed the time as you sat in misery on that poor toilet we are happy to keep your money. No matter what the case, if you learned a little, laughed a little and survived to drink again another day, our job is done.

Come meet us at the bar and you can buy us a drink.

"Health – what my friends are
always drinking to before they fall down."
~ Phyllis Diller

David Sloan
We hope these beer companies appreciate the free advertising

Drinking
Activity
Guide
*Easy ways to have
fun with your booze!*

About Our Friends

Did you notice a few advertisements at the bottoms of the pages or are you still too hungover? These are our friends and they hooked us up by sponsoring the book. Read all about them in the pages that follow and you will see why we love them. After that, check them out in person and you will love them too. If you live in Key West and are upset because your business isn't listed, invite us out for a beer. If we hit it off, you might make the next printing.

Pirate Scooter 305.295.0000

Put on the brakes, baby! We are not saying you should ride a scooter while drinking, drunk or even hungover, but after reading this guide hangovers will be a thing of the past and there is no better way to spend the day than tooling around town on a Pirate Scooter. Let us reiterate: Scooters should be driven in complete sobriety with all of your senses intact. Fixing a broken scooter is expensive, but not nearly as expensive as fixing a broken spine. Pirate Scooter is our favorite place, mostly because our friend Brett owns it and he has nice teeth. He also sells our books from his stand and here at Phantom Press we are not above shameless promotion to pay for our next drink. We are also big pirate fans and have the fashion sense to know that nothing goes better with a scooter than an eye patch and buccaneer hat. If you don't feel like walking, give Pirate Scooter a call and Brett will deliver a two-wheeled galleon to your door. Be sure to compliment him on his pearly whites.

> "Well I woke up Sunday morning with
> no way to hold my head that didn't hurt.
> And the beer I had for breakfast wasn't bad
> so I had one more for dessert."
> ~ Kris Kristofferson - Sunday Morning Coming Down

Planet Smoothie
1075 Duval Street, 305.294.4604 www.PlanetSmoothie.com

The ultimate way to start your day is with a delicious frozen fruit smoothie! Equipped with everything your body needs to get back up to par, Planet Smoothie has every fruit combination under the sun with vitamin and mineral supplements that will whisk your hangover away. You cannot go wrong with Chris's favorite, the Hangover Over. It lives up to the name. David is a fan of the blueberry-banana-mango-protein powder combo, but both agree that Susan is the best smoothie-maker in town. Her smile will take the edge off your hangover while she mixes up the delicious smoothie goodness.

Grand Vin
1107 Duval Street, 305.296.1020

This fabulous wine shop and drinkery is a throwback to how bars used to be. Classy at times, rarely serious and never pretentious, a good time is always waiting for you at The Vin. Choose a wine by the glass from their menu or select a bottle from their extensive collection and open it there. Prepare yourself for local theatrics as the regulars, owners and bartenders, rant and rave about everything from politics to new sexual techniques. If you are lucky, you might even see Chris here.

Lazy Gecko
203 Duval Street. 305.292.1903 www.TheLazyGecko.com

Do you ladies like to dance on bars? Do you guys like to watch ladies dancing on bars? Do any of you like to watch the people watching the people dancing on bars? The Lazy Gecko has something for everybody. Just about anything goes and nobody talks about it the next day. Strong drinks and a sexy staff make this the ideal bar to plant yourself in for several hours and it has a prime location on lower Duval Street that fits perfectly with your bar crawl. Right next door to Sloppy Joe's, the Gecko has specialty drinks galore. Try the O'Gasm or Lady Godzilla and you will understand why dancing on the floor just doesn't cut it. Guys should try Hemingway's favorite drink, the Bacardi Mojito. Resist the urge to ask sexy bartenders if they are on the menu. We tried that line and it does not work. Did we mention the pizza? Mmmm, pizza.

Cafe Solé

1029 Southard Street 305.294.0230 www.CafeSole.com

Would you like to know a secret? Promise you won't tell? Okay, you can tell. It is the least we can do since you shelled out some cash for our book. But if you are reading someone else's copy we expect a check from you for the little tidbit we are about to share. In Key West, restaurants on Duval Street will always survive because they get tons of walk-by traffic. Great ones thrive, bad ones survive. Restaurants off the beaten path don't make it more than a year if they don't have something special. Cafe Solé has been in business for over 10 years! Chef John Correa fine tuned his cooking skills in France, opened the restaurant with his wife Judy (at the corner of Southard and Frances) and combined his mastery of sauces with local seafood to create dishes that are out of this world. If we could get more dates we would eat here every night, but we settle for the Sunday Brunch which, if we still got hangovers, would cure them in no time. The hogfish is famous, the lobster bisque will blow you out of the water, and the prices are fair. John has won so many awards we are surprised he has room in the kitchen to store food. Zagats rated Cafe Solé the best food in the Florida Keys. Somebody get us a date.

Ok, class, today we'll be sitting quietly
with the lights off because teacher
has a hangover.
~ Edna Krabappel

Monsoon Café
829 Fleming St., 305.29CAMEL www.MonsoonCafe.net

We have been bitching for a combined total of 17 years about the lack of curry joints in Key West. You may not realize how much you crave curry in the big city when it is readily available, but down here in the tropics we want some curry and we want it now. Luckily the good folks at Monsoon Café listened to the pleas of our curryless citizens and went balls to the wall. We now have enough varieties to keep our tongues tingling into the next millennium. Our favorite one is made with Guinness Beer and it is friggin' hot! One bite had our mouths burning with flavor and we couldn't stop until the dish was gone. There wasn't even time to drink beer until our plates were clean, our eyes were watering and we felt like we had just had sex. (but not with each other.) Curry isn't the only thing here. They have a great selection of Oriental and Indian fusion, but we loved the curry so much we get it every time. There is a laundromat next door, so if you drank too much last night and got sick on your clothes, clean them up next door and cure your hangover with some of the best curry this side of the Equator.

The Banyan Resort
323 Whitehead Street, 866.371.9222,
www.TheBanyanResort.com

When our family and friends come to town we don't let them stay with us. They drink all of our beer, make us do laundry and think we are up for a drink 24 hours a day. We are up for the drinks, but we prefer to do it on their dime at the Banyan Resort. The Banyan is in the heart of Old Town and only steps from the

"Drink the first.
Sip the second slowly.
Skip the third."
~ Knute Rockne

best bars on Duval Street. This means the party and the tranquil tropical courtyard outside of your room are only separated by a two-minute walk. Most of the Banyan's guests never want to leave, so they offer timeshare re-sales without the aggressive pitch. The tiki bar and Jacuzzi make it one of our favorite places for happy hour with our guests, and we always seem to make new friends when we are there. This place is all about luxury. Even if you don't stay here, take a walk down Whitehead Street and check out the banyan trees in the front yard. Banyans drop roots that become tree trunks and the suckers just keep expanding. These are some of the largest banyan trees on the island (hence the name of the resort) and they are spectacular. Resist the urge to climb them. You will fall down. We speak from experience.

Conch Republic Seafood Company
631 Greene Street, 305.294.4403,
www.ConchRepublicSeafood.com

Adam and Eve would be jealous. This place is a giant open-air warehouse-turned-restaurant with an oval-shaped bar that is nothing less than massive. Seafood galore, a selection of over 80 rums and an antique 1,200-pound copper still are just the start.

The Conch Farm (as locals call it) offers prime viewing of the hustle and bustle in the Historic Seaport, has a happy hour that will knock your socks off and is just a few short steps away from Jimmy Buffett's recording studio. The same bartenders have been there for years so you can expect a familiar face every time you return. We drink there frequently so it is a good spot to find us if

> "Of the demonstrably wise there are but two: those who commit suicide, and those who keep their 20 reasoning faculties atrophied by drink."
> ~Mark Twain, Note-Book, 1935

you need an autograph for your book. They sell our books there too, so don't hesitate to pick up additional copies for your friends.

The Southernmost Scavenger Hunt (Best of the Bars)
430 Duval Street , 305.292.9994, www.KeyWestHunt.com

Our friend Graff and his wife Eileen started this tour and it has exploded. The Classic Scavenger Hunt lets you compete against other teams for prizes and gives you a chance to experience the parts of Key West you are not likely to stumble upon with your free map. We love the Classic Hunt, but usually opt for the Best of the Bars. It's much like the classic but we get to drink more. Everyone gets together at the top of the La Concha Hotel. If you can't find it you are doing a fine job of drinking. It is the tallest building in town and located smack, dab in the middle of Duval Street. Give Graff a call for a one-of-a-kind experience that is Key West to the core.

Fat Tuesday
305 Duval Street, 305.296.9373,
www.FatTuesdayKeyWest.com

The 300 block of Duval Street could be one of the most dangerous areas in town. It has nothing to do with crime, we just can't seem to walk past Fat Tuesday without stopping in for one of their frozen drinks. The Key West Fat Tuesday is unlike any other. You have a full bar with the frozen drinks as a specialty and good-looking people hanging all around, but this is the only Fat Tuesday that also features the daily parade of characters on Duval Street and the Key West breezes. The frozen drink options run higher than we can count and you can mix and match to create your own special treat. Try the 190 Octane and your day will not be the same. Try more and you might not make it to sunset. Say hi to ChaChi.

Martin's
416 Applerouth Lane, 305.296.1183, www.Martins-Cafe.com

Our favorite place in the world for eggs benedict happens to be right down the street from where we live. Martin's adds secret German ingredients and, what we can only assume is, a touch of crack to his hollandaise sauce. Whatever it is, we are addicted. There is something about brunch at Martin's that makes it more than an eating experience. Not only is the food delectable, but you leave feeling high and mighty. Martin's is no one trick pony. They offer fine European dining at night that our friends who have dates can't stop talking about. Martin did this place up right with the choice of indoor seating or dining under the stars. An excellent selection of beer and wine and a sexy German accent make Martin's one of our favorite stops when we want to get it on.

Solar Spa
2824 North Roosevelt Blvd., 305.295.7177, www.KeyWester.info

We don't care if you have the worst hangover of your life or if you've never taken a sip of alcohol. If you want to feel good, good, good, treat yourself to one of the several pampering treatments at The Solar Spa. Get a tan, enjoy a massage, try out some microdermabrasion or relax with a nice facial. Hair of the dog may cure your hangover, but ladies, that is also a term we guys use for your unsightly mustache. Get it removed at the solar spa and don't be afraid to go Brazilian. Before you guys start cracking jokes, try a pedicure. Your feet are horrible and nail treatments are not just for women anymore. Don't go for the pink nail polish, but try a manicure and pedicure and the women will adore you.

915
915 Duval Street, 305.296.0669, www.NineOneFive.com

We were excited to hear they were opening a topless restaurant on Duval Street, but a little embarrassed when we went to 915's grand opening with an arm full of beads. We drank too much that day and confused "tapas" with "topless." Luckily the owners and staff were gracious and forgiving of our mistake and 915 has become one of our favorite spots. 915 has taken dining to the next level. Order several appetizers, order dessert before dinner, eat the traditional way or just chill with a bottle of wine. It is your dining experience and they want you to do what you please. The food is out of this world and the wine selection second to none. Over 30 wines by the glass make for a selection that rivals regions of France and the atmosphere is classy and elegant.

Great place to take your date, just make sure you ennuciate "tapas" correctly.

Island Joe's Coffee
islandjoesgourmetcoffee.com

When you drink as much booze as we do, you end up knocking back a lot of coffee to get fueled up for that thing we call work. Some nationally franchised coffee shops have moved to Key West in the last few years, and though we welcome them to our tiny island, when it's time to indulge in a fresh brew we visit our friend Island Joe. Joe is a real person and we have known him for years. He has a passion for coffee that verges on insanity and if you have the good fortune to meet him in person it will be a conversation that you won't soon forget. Track him down in town or order his coffee on the internet. If you can find a better cup of coffee anywhere we will eat this book. (after soaking the pages in Island Joe's coffee, of course.)

Hangover Ratings

This next little gem has been making the rounds on the internet. We are glad to see someone knows hangovers nearly as well as we do. If you created this beauty, let us know. We will put you in the next printing and guarantee your place in the hangover hall of fame.

One Star Hangover (*)

No pain. No real feeling of illness. You're able to function relatively well. However, you are parched. You can drink five sodas and still feel this way. For some reason, you are craving a steak and fries.

Two Star Hangover (**)

No pain, but something is definitely amiss. You may look okay, but you have the mental capacity of a staple gun. The coffee you are chugging is only increasing your rumbling gut, which is still tossing around the fruity pancake from the 3 a.m. Waffle House excursion. There is some definite havoc being wreaked upon your bowels.

Three Star Hangover (***)

Slight headache. Stomach feels crappy. You are definitely not productive. Anytime a girl walks by you gag because her perfume reminds you of the flavored schnapps shots your alcoholic friends dared you to drink. Life would be better right now if you were home in your bed watching Lucy reruns. You've had 4 cups of coffee, a gallon of water, three iced teas and a Diet Coke – yet you haven't peed once.

Four Star Hangover (****)

Life sucks. Your head is throbbing. You can't speak too quickly or you might puke. Your boss has already lambasted you for being late and has given you a lecture for reeking of booze. You wore nice clothes, but that can't hide the fact that you only shaved one side of your face (for the ladies, it looks like you put your make-up on while riding bumper cars). Your eyes look like one big red vein, and even your hair hurts. Your sphincter is in perpetual spasm, and the first of about five dumps you take during the day brings water to the eyes of everyone who enters the bathroom.

Five Star Hangover (*****)

You have a second heartbeat in your head, which is actually annoying the employee who sits in the next cube. Vodka vapor is seeping out of every pore and making you dizzy. You still have toothpaste crust in the corners of your mouth from brushing your teeth in an attempt to get the remnants of the poop fairy out. Your body has lost the ability to generate saliva so your tongue is suffocating you. Any attempt to defecate results in a fire-hose-like discharge of alcohol-scented fluid with a rare 'floater' thrown in. The sole purpose of this 'floater' seems to be to splash the toilet water all over your bum. You are thinking that death might be better than this...

Spice Things Up!

For loved ones, your hangover loses all comedic value the moment your stomach empties her contents. The headache, weary eyes and lack of posture tickled a funny bone somewhere, but walrus screams and buffalo moans coming from the bathroom will zap the humor out of any situation. If you insist on bringing the entire situation down to your level, have some class and avoid clichés such as "I'm gonna be sick" or "time to blow chunks." Celebrate putting your face where countless asses have been by using one of the descriptive terms below, compliments of the Vomit Thesaurus.

Put out the fire with Barfalo Bill
Argue with the worms
Take the Big Spit
Visit the bile geyser
Take a chow shower
Go chumming
Deliver a street pizza
Jazz up the carpet
Leggo of your Eggo
Sing a rainbow
Burp in 3-D
Milk the brown cow
Throw it in reverse
Spray puree
Buy a round-trip meal ticket
Go for a second chew
Scream in Technicolor
Do the Hoaky Croaky

That's what it's all about!

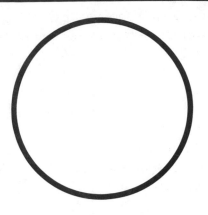

DO NOT DISTURB!

KEY WEST HANGOVER IN PROGRESS

Cut out this bad boy and hang it on your door.

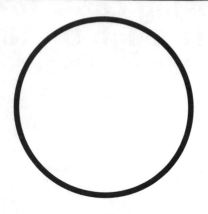

GONE DRINKING!

I READ THE KEY WEST HANGOVER SURVIVAL GUIDE!

Drinking Cards To Get You Through the Night. Cut them out and hit the town!

Please Shut Up

The presenter of this card is suffering from an excruciating hangover. Though they brought this pain upon themselves, at this time they cannot come up with a tactful way to ask you to shut the hell up. If you would be so kind as to stop speaking for an extended period of time, your present company would be most appreciative.

www.phantompress.com

Shotgun

The bearer of this card is entitled to ride "shotgun" even if someone else called it first. They are suffering from a major hangover making them ineligible to operate a motor vehicle, but highly qualified for control of the air conditioner and stereo system. Shotgun may be modified to include sleeping in the backseat at the bearer's discretion, provided the new front seat passenger adheres to a/c and stereo requests.

www.phantompress.com

Bartender's Choice

Dear Bartender:
This person is too hungover to speak and would like some hair of the dog. Please speak gently, move quickly and whip up the finest hangover cure in the bar. Money is not an issue and they will thank you just as soon as their cognitive skills return.

www.phantompress.com

Drinking Cards To Get You Through the Night. Cut them out and hit the town!

Get Me Some Water

Upon receiving this card, you are instructed to obtain a glass of water for the person who presented the card. Bottled water is preferred. Delivery of water which has not been chilled or served over ice is punishable by a trip to the store for ice cream. Failure to provide a minimum of 18 ounces will result in the severing of all ties. This card can only be used by the original presenter so don't try to use it on them.

www.phantompress.com

Bathroom V.I.P.

This card entitles the bearer to all benefits associated with the bathroom including, but not limited to, first dibs, last clean towel, unlimited hot water, use of another person's toothbrush, forgetting to flush, leaving the seat up and falling asleep in the shower. If this card is slipped under the bathroom door, the bathroom occupant is required to tidy up quickly and vacate the bathroom immediately.

www.phantompress.com

Hangover Helper

The person who handed you this card noticed you were hungover or at the very least look like hell. Do yourself a favor and pick up a copy of The Key West Hangover Survival Guide. It is carb-free, low in fat and will help to cure what ales ya. Pick one up in any local bookstore or gift shop, or order online. Buy one for all of your alcoholic friends.

www.phantompress.com

Hangover Cards To Ease The Pain. No need to talk if you have these!

Get Out Of Jail Free

This card entitles the bearer to be released from police custody upon apologizing for their drunken antics and promising to go straight home, never letting something like this to happen again. Card may only be used in Key West, Florida. Effectiveness may vary depending on blood alcohol level and arresting officer's mood. Attempts to use this card by sober people will render it null and void.

www.phantompress.com

THE **HANGOVER** SURVIVAL GUIDE

Thank You Bartender

Present this card to your favorite bartender to let them know how much you appreciate their excellent service. If this card is accompanied by a nice tip the bartender will agree to provide you with more excellent service and might even buy you a shot. If this card is used in place of a tip you can expect to be ignored and possibly shot.

www.phantompress.com

THE **HANGOVER** SURVIVAL GUIDE

Have Sex With Me Please

The person who handed you this card is obviously very drunk, desperate and horny. They couldn't even read the small print explaining what a loser they are. It is unlikely they will be able to find their way home, much less perform in bed, but if you have a warm spot in your heart for pitiful people, please consider taking them home and showing them a good time.

www.phantompress.com

THE **HANGOVER** SURVIVAL GUIDE

Hangover Cards To Ease The Pain. No need to talk if you have these!

Don't Kick My Ass

Please don't kick the bearer of this card's ass. They may be drunk, stupid, obnoxious and belligerent, but they need love and a warm bed to sleep in more than a cracked rib and a broken collar bone. You can obviously take them, so let's just chalk up a win for you and call it a night. Fighting a drunk person may be humorous but where is the challenge?

www.phantompress.com

Please Get Me Home

Lick the back of this card and stick it on your forehead prior to passing out.

Drop Me Off At:

_____

your address here

www.phantompress.com

Sorry For The Mess

The person who left this card would like to apologize for the mess they have left in your establishment. Be it a broken bottle, spilled beer, torn up bar coasters, a urine soaked toilet seat or an explosion of vomit. They have chosen to remain anonymous because they are easily embarrassed but would like to assure you that they don't usually behave in this manner. Thank you for your understanding.

www.phantompress.com

The Magic Dot

A Buddhist monk recently spoke in Key West and we attended in hopes of finding spiritual enlightenment. As soon as he mentioned dharma we started thinking about Jenna Elfman and the rest of his talk was a blur. In hopes of getting something in return for our $12 donation, we asked the wise man about Tibetan hangover cures. He gave us this dot. Follow the instructions – it may work for you.

Instructions: Focus on the center of the circle with your heart and your mind. After several moments the magic will come to you and your hangover will be cured.

About Christopher Shultz

Chris has lived, worked and drank in Key West for some time now. He will probably be there for a while or at least until something better comes along. He likes to drink moderately almost every day keeping a constant balance between beer, coffee, pot and cigarettes. He has quit all three several times only to go running back to them like a little girl who misses her mommy. He has dreams of lots of things. Most involve Tinkerbell, a bottle of Stoli and a hammock.

Chris would like to thank everybody who has bought or served him a drink, sold him a bag or bummed him a cigarette. Special thanks to Jodi, his mom, his dog Jonci, and David for putting up with him on a daily basis and still talking to him.

Chris' Hangover History

First Hangover: 9th grade, after binging on Southern Comfort and Lemonade. I puked my guts out and spent the entire day hiding under my covers wishing I was dead. Thank God there was a marathon of "Gentle Ben" to soothe me through the day.

Worst Hangover: A half bottle of absinthe seemed like a good idea at the time. The next day I woke up in Kmart clutching a six pack, some fresh underwear and an X-Men DVD. My eyeballs rolled all the way down aisle 10. Someone brought me home and I dry heaved for six hours. Happy Thanksgiving.

Longest Hangover: Five Thousand Seven Hundred Sixty Minutes.

Hangover Helper: Grilled cheese, a beer and a stripper.

Hangover Achievements: I've puked at four state fairs.

Hangover Hell: Catholic church service. The incense they use makes me want to puke. Especially hungover at a funeral.

Hangover Heaven: When my mom gives me a bong hit and a sandwich.

Great Moments in Drinking: Telling a marine in full camouflage that I was very impressed with his floating head. It was nice to see the government spend money on such great camouflage. I challenged his head to a fight, just me and the head. His head kicked my ass. Lesson learned; don't pick on people in camouflage. They can kick your ass.

Favorite Drinks: Beer, wine, vodka, absinthe. In no particular order.

About David Sloan

David L. Sloan began drinking in Wayne, Pennsylvania at age twelve after playing Zeppelin IV backwards at a loud volume. He continued to practice his craft through high school and college with a major in drunkenness and a minor in debauchery, yet somehow managed a successful stint in the corporate world and started multiple businesses in the Keys. Living in Key West pushed his drinking achievements to an all time high and Sloan was able to tie the island's record for "most consecutive days without sobriety". He now lives in Key West with his macaw, T.J. and cat, Dr. Jekyll. All three are recovering alcoholics.

David would like to thank Christopher Shultz and everyone reading this who is looking for their name mentioned in thanks. You know who you are.

David's Hangover History

First Hangover: Unable to recall due to memory loss.

Worst Hangover: An ounce of gin for each of my years seemed like a good idea at sixteen. Forty-eight hours of dry heaves reminded me it was not.

Longest Hangover: Four days that felt like a week.

Hangover Helper: Soft Pretzels with melted cheese, club soda, bitters and a vitamin B shot.

Hangover Achievements: I've thrown up in 17 different countries.

Hangover Hell: I came to in a Mexican jail after a night that included more tequila shots than I can count on both hands and an arrest for urinating in public. The jail floor was flooded with sewage and insects avoided the flood by using my ears as an ark. The Mexican guards apparently had no comprehension of the term "liquid refreshment" in either Spanish or English.

Hangover Heaven: I told my dentist about a hangover and he pumped me full of laughing gas. Hangover cured.

Great Moments in Drinking: I once fell out of a moving station wagon without spilling my beer.

Favorite drink: Miller Lite in a bottle with a splash of good lovin'.

Also available from Phantom Press
www.phantompress.com

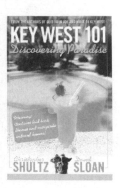
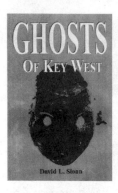

Also available from Phantom Press
www.phantompress.com

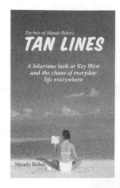
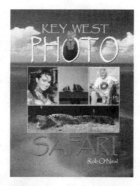

Discount pricing available when you buy 10 copies or more.
Email direct@phantompress.com

Sign up for the free Phantom Press newsletter at
www.phantompress.com

The authors are available for book signings, corporate events
or keg parties. For more information contact
bookings@phantompress.com

Why are you still reading this?
The book is over. Go out and have a drink.